Death
Til the End

GLENDA BARNETT-STREICHER

Mother to domestic violence
Victim Rebecca "Becca" Ollis-Coons

authorHOUSE®

AuthorHouse™
1663 Liberty Drive
Bloomington, IN 47403
www.authorhouse.com
Phone: 1-800-839-8640

First published by AuthorHouse 1/27/2011

ISBN: 978-1-4567-2472-6 (dj)
ISBN: 978-1-4567-2473-3 (e)
ISBN: 978-1-4567-2474-0 (sc)

Library of Congress Control Number: 2011900469

Printed in the United States of America

Preface

Rebecca Lynn Ollis was born on April 24, 1972, a beautiful Monday evening, the little sister to Lisa Marie. Becca was the mother of TJ, born October 1991, and Leslie Ann, born October 1993. My first book "Finding the Me in Me, Do You Know the You in You?" was published in December 2009, and is about how I felt my role as a parent impacted her life and decisions.

After her murder on Friday November 09, 2007, I felt if there was any way to help others understand the process of what you have to go through I will have served part of my purpose and role in bringing her killer to justice. Therefore, this is being written with the hopes of helping some other family member as they travel through the court process within our legal justice system. The challenge of not knowing what is going to happen next and still living each day with just getting by is by far the hardest thing I have ever had to do. As a part of the total process we must deal with the death of our loved one, while also finding our own coping mechanisms for survival.

We are so often prejudiced by television shows that we think the world moves as the shows we watch. Believe me that is not the case. As pre-warned by the Assistant District Attorney, the usual time for a murder trial is a minimum of two years and more often than not, it may actually be longer. So whatever you do, don't take literally what you see on Law and Order or Criminal Intent – that truly is not the real world or anywhere close to it - it is Hollywood.

There are times you feel that nothing is happening and in fact it may not be, but you must be patient and wait for the process to occur. It is important to find something with meaning for yourself to focus on, to get through the times of waiting. My out is writing. Yours may be singing, painting, or even dancing. It doesn't matter what it is just find that 'out'. So as we journey through the legal component, we also journey through coping with death and dying. I hope these words will make a difference, will help you in times of frustration to know the process will happen it just takes time. Above all else don't forget to take the opportunity daily to talk with God and ask Him for strength you may need to make it through another day or most importantly just thank Him for being there.

Dedication

To Susan Tucker and Katie Miller of the Nashville, Tennessee, District Attorney's office who were not only the legal team and professionals at my side, but became my friends at a time when you feel most alone.

To Pat Shea the Director, Mary Jones a survivor, and all the staff of my new found family from the Middle Tennessee YWCA and Weaver Domestic Violence Center, who though Becca never got the chance to know them, have given me strength and purpose in the loss of my daughter.

Most of all to Joseph, my husband, Lisa my daughter, and my grandchildren – TJ, Leslie, Kayla, Christian, and Joshua, who give me love and strength to get up each morning and face the world knowing they are in it.

A special thank you goes to Rose Lubbert, Nurse Educator in Omaha, Nebraska, and Reba Barnes of Joelton, Tennessee, who each graciously took on the task of reviewing my writing and offered valuable input. To Jan Combs a person who will forever have a special place in my heart for being there for me and to all those who shared their experiences and thoughts when dealing with death of their own loved one, I thank you.

Contents

CHAPTER ONE

The Beginning

In the beginning God created the heaven and the earth, and the earth was without form, and void; and darkness was upon the face of the deep. And the Spirit of God moved upon the face of the waters. And God said, Let there be light; and there was light. And God saw the light, that it was good; and God divided the light from the darkness. And God called the light Day and the darkness he called Night. And the evening and the morning were the first day. Genesis 1: 1-5 KJV

There is always a beginning to everything. As we waken each morning we know not what lies ahead. The kind of night we had affects what we have to look forward to and what our reaction to the day will be. We open our eyes to prepare for day, dressing for work, getting kids ready and to school, making phone calls to outline all that is on our calendar, and in general just facing the day with most often a decent attitude. I have come to live by the rule that today may in fact be the last day of my life and try to do what God would expect and set an example for those around me. You see my life changed forever just a few short years ago and that is the story I share with you now.

> ***Friday morning November 9, 2007***, at 1:05 a.m. I received a phone call from Thomas Coons. ***"Well he did it – Jimmy killed Becca."***

I'll forever and ever hear those words in my head. Thomas-Jimmy's brother- explained to me that Jimmy had called him from a pay phone and asked that he and his mom come pick him up. Once they got him they drove back to the apartment, where according to Thomas he tried to do CPR on Becca, but couldn't save her and that the paramedics were with her at the time. I screamed at him and called him a liar, told him that this was a cruel joke, until he let me talk to the EMT who confirmed my baby was dead. I then asked God to care for her and to give me strength to forgive. Nothing in my world will ever be the same again.

In order to begin this chronological accounting of the trial process and how coping became a part of my life, the events leading up to it and the first days need to be documented as well.

By profession I am a Registered Nurse and frequently travel as a part of my job. When I received the early morning phone call I was in Shelby, North Carolina, a drive of approximately eight to nine hours or a short plane ride away from my home in Nashville, Tennessee. I was scheduled to return home late that Friday afternoon, but of course I couldn't wait. I had to get home to Becca. I couldn't think straight, much less phantom attempting to drive that distance. I already had a flight for my return trip home. Could it be changed, who was with Becca, what had he done, why was this happening? There were so many thoughts running through my head and I really didn't know what to do first. As previously stated my thoughts went to God – to take care of my baby, to give me strength to forgive and to give guidance to make a difference in another's life because of what Becca had suffered.

I first called my husband – Doc, he had to go be with Becca, I didn't want her alone, then my pastor - Buddy, then the Administrator of the clinics I was visiting on this trip – Jan. Jan was going to call and change my flight home and then come to the hotel where I was. All I could do was pick up clothes and throw them in the suitcase and pace the floor. Who could I talk to, who did I need to talk to? Then it hit me - I better tell the clerk at the desk to expect Jan so they would let her in, after all it was 1:30 in the morning. Had to call Lisa (my older daughter) she had to know, then call my boss and call Tim and Sue they would have to tell Leslie and TJ –Becca's daughter and son. Oh, God what about the kids?

Jan was able to get me on a flight and back to Nashville by 8:30 a.m. As would be expected there were minutes of tears, and just withdrawal – I was alone like my baby was. How could I just be sitting and waiting and not be moving? When was the plane going to leave? It had to hurry and get me there, no delays were allowed. The flight gate attendant saw I was crying and asked if she could help. I explained my baby had just been murdered and I had to get home to Nashville. When the plane finally arrived at the gate they boarded me first. I was able to sit alone on this early morning flight. I remember looking out the windows at the clouds and in my mind actually seeing Becca dancing there. The clouds appeared to be soft and fluffy, pure white and to be open with beauty. The back ground was the most beautiful shade of blue – soothing. Throughout the flight of only about 45 minutes the flight attendant would come back and hold my hand and talk to me.

Finally, I got to Nashville. I still had to get my luggage from baggage claim and go to my awaiting husband. Becca lived close to the airport so my first trip was to her apartment. There was no where else I wanted to be. Adrenalin was rushing through my body, as were the thoughts in my head. Never before had the ride to her apartment seemed so long. The door to the apartment had a biohazard sign. They had removed her body just a short time before I arrived. I can't imagine my baby lying on that hard floor for over seven hours. Who was in her house going through her things, trying to figure out what had happened? The apartment supervisor said I couldn't go in yet, that the crime scene hadn't been released. I just wanted to hold Becca…was she warm, were they being kind to her? Why couldn't I have gotten there sooner? If I had just seen her before they took her away.

On the ride from the airport, Doc didn't talk at first, allowing me to just think and not question if I was okay because it was a given fact no mother would be okay when her baby was dead. When I finally got up the nerve to ask questions he filled me in as to what he had seen when he got to the apartment before the police took Jimmy. He made it clear to me that Thomas had no blood on his clothing or hands so he could not have tried to do CPR on Becca. There was a large amount of blood from the wounds so if he had in fact tried to save her, there would have been blood on his hands or clothes. Guess he just wanted me to think he was some sort of hero – fat chance, I know his history. There had been TV coverage because it was a stabbing and of course the media covers all the bad stuff in the world. I think we need some good news coverage once in awhile. That isn't really fair to them because they are the local news and murders are news. They released Becca's name about eight that morning after the medical examiner had gotten there and the body had been released to the morgue. When asked why it had taken so long to get the scene processed and Becca moved, it was stated that there had been another murder about the same time that had tied up the coroner.

Doc explained to me that Jimmy is the one that actually called the police. He had evidently called his mom and brother first, and then, after Thomas and his mom picked him up, they went back to the apartment, the call was made to the police and the three awaited their arrival. I called Thomas and Donna after landing, to let them know I was there and on my way to the apartment. They were also on their way back to the apartment with a truck to start moving things out. Thomas said the supervisor at the apartment told him everything had to be out by midnight. Can you believe that? My baby was dead and all they cared about was vacating the apartment.

With the biohazard sign on the door, we had the supervisor of the apartment complex contact the police to see when we could enter the apartment. They advised her they had all the information they needed so it was okay for us to move whatever needed to be moved – which was everything since we had a midnight deadline. Everyone else went in first to see what needed to be shielded from me. They tried to cover the blood on the kitchen\dining room floor with trash bags so I wouldn't see it. Duh, how obvious does a trash bag make things look? Did they think I wouldn't pay attention? I knew my baby had died in that apartment and I was ready to walk thru the door and take what I needed for the moment.

Once Thomas got there I couldn't think about what I really wanted and didn't want, so I grabbed a few things – wallet, Becca's Dale Earnhardt coat, mom's sewing machine, key chain that said **"*speak out against domestic violence*"**, a few other items and told them to do whatever they wanted with everything else. I couldn't deal with it right then. I had no doubt they had planned to claim everything as Jimmy's anyway. I didn't have use for her clothes so I just let them clean up the mess and take everything. Looking at her wallet which had her bank account information, the first thing Doc and I did was go to the bank to close the account, to the post office to cancel her PO Box and then to the funeral home. It's interesting that when we got to the funeral home and started filling out papers one of the things we had to do was to provide information for the Obituary. I remembered to mention her Nanny and Pappy (dad's parents) who are both deceased, but it has since been called to my attention that I totally forgot to even mention her biological father. He just simply did not come to mind because he had chosen not to be a part of her life. It wasn't an intentional oversight, it just didn't happen.

Doc talked about how he wished he had killed Jimmy, that he was supposed to take care of family and he hadn't. I thanked God that he hadn't carried through those thoughts because then he would be in jail instead of Jimmy. Since Jimmy was in jail somebody had to handle things and she was my baby so I took control. I would hate to think what would have transpired had someone told me I couldn't. They always say you should never cross a mother and her cubs – well this was <u>my baby cub</u>. I was her mother and I had to take care of her, it was the last thing I could do for her.

That first day was pretty much a blur of details, just getting family in, making phone calls, and doing a lot of wandering around doing nothing. Lisa (Becca's sister) was on her way from North Carolina, my mom was in Knoxville so Lisa would stop and tell her and then bring her to Nashville also. The medical examiner was supposed to release the body to the funeral home about 4:30 p.m. They had to do an autopsy because of it being a murder. Wish I didn't know all the details about autopsies – all the TV programs cover them and I am a nurse with basic knowledge.

You always hear the body is treated with respect so you have to believe that. The autopsy process then means I won't be able to see her until tomorrow, I just need to go to her, I need to hold her and let her know I am here. The police say she died instantly and didn't suffer, but how do they know? They weren't there and it sure wasn't them, they don't know what she was feeling. I remember from TV shows how families go to the morgue to identify the body. I suppose that due to Jimmy being on site that no one needed to identify her, but I wanted to go to her and I couldn't.

As that first evening back at home without my baby in the world began I found myself at a loss of what I was supposed to be doing. If I had arrived home at my normal time then I would probably be on the phone right now telling Becca all about my week and finding out what she had been doing. Our usual routine was to talk at least once while I was away and then when I got home so she knew I was back and safe and I knew she was okay. Mom, Lisa, and Doc were all at the house with me, but no one was really taking control of conversations. I remember there was food prepared but as could be expected food was not on my mind.

I had thousands of thoughts going through my head, but none connect with each other. I felt I had to do something to figure out what had gone on.

Our wonderful world of technology allowed me to go on line to the Metro Nashville Police Department website and obtain a copy of the Media Release. It was strange reading on a website, actions that had happened to your own daughter. It also listed a lengthy arrest history which included aggravated assault for kicking and punching Rebecca Coons in the face in November 2002. Not my daughter, but his first wife. I had never known his prior wife was named Rebecca also. He was convicted of misdemeanor domestic assault and ordered to spend six months in jail. Again in August 2005 he was arrested for harassing his wife – again not my Becca. I think this time it might have been even another wife. James Coons III according to the media release is being held in lieu of $500,000 bond on a charge of criminal homicide. I wish now I had thought to check police website before Becca ever married him in 2006.

> *Yea, though I walk through the valley of the shadow of death, I will fear no evil; for You are with me; Your rod and Your staff, they comfort me. Thou preparest a table before me in the presence of mine enemies; Thou anointest my head with oil; my cup runneth over. Surley goodness and mercy shall follow me all the days of my life; and I will dwell in the house of the Lord forever.* Psalms 23:4-6 KJV

Death is final, no matter what your beliefs may be. Death is final, for the human body. The spirit then takes its place in heaven if you are a believer of God, as Becca and I are. Others are entitled to have their own beliefs. I would say to you to know that the way to heaven is through Jesus Christ and the day will come when I meet not only my Jesus but my family again.

What is important to remember is the human body ceases to be as it has always been known, no matter what your belief may be. How do you begin to cope with that death, that loss, that person you can no longer reach out and touch, or tell your darkest secrets to? No matter the age of the person, the gender, or the relationship, all people that had a chance to know the person will be impacted to some degree. I think what I miss the most is her sweet voice saying "I just wanted to talk to my mommy." I heard her voice over and over in my head, the words that are so dear to any mother, and these were actually the last words I heard her say.

Grief and Loss Expert, Dr. Kirsti A. Dyer advised that "**Sometime the best you can hope to do during times of challenge is remember the basics and take things one minute at time, one hour at a time, one day at a time.**"

When faced with a loss, a significant life change or a death, one of the greatest challenges for the person is figuring out what to do to make it through the first few hours and the first few days.

TAKE CARE of Yourself

The TAKE CARE acronym was developed by Dr. Dyer to be a useful reminder that helps grieving people focus on the basics following a loss, a death or other when grieving any significant life changing event.

- Time is needed to handle the grief.

- Avoid alcohol and other medications.
- Keep to some routine or schedule.
- Eat a balanced diet. Focus on healthy foods and water.
- Converse with others, especially those that have "been there" and "survived that."
- Art projects can keep worried hands busy, whether journaling, building, crafting, knitting or in other ways.
- Rest and Sleep are important to help the body heal.
- Exercise to reduce stress and improve one's mood.

These are the areas that a person needs to focus on during the initial shock phase, when coming to grips with a loss or death.

Remember to Breathe

In addition to taking care of oneself, it is also helpful during times when things get to be overwhelming to remember a simple mantra and breathe...just breathe. Using this simple mantra can be a helpful way to calm oneself during times of anxiety or stress.

How Sudden Death Differs from Normal Grief

For the family left behind, coping with the loss of a child due to a sudden cause can be very difficult. The grief response following sudden loss is often intensified since there is no opportunity to prepare for the loss or say good-bye. The shock and grief following a sudden death can be overwhelming.

Coping with the Sudden Death of a Child

The Compassionate Friends offer some helpful insights into

understanding the emotional response that parents face following the sudden death of a child based on the early works of John Bowlby and Colin Murray Parkes:

- *Shock* is frequently the initial response to sudden bad news along with numbness.
- *Guilt and Anger* are emotions common for parents, particularly if they felt that there was something they could have done or someone else could have done to prevent the death.
- *Accepting the Reality* may be very difficult for parents. They may experience intense yearning and longing for the child who has died. Finding ways to remember the child can be helpful.
- *Reorganizing and Readjusting* involves living through the grief, reorganizing their lives, readjusting to a world without their child and finding a new normal.

Sudden Death is a Traumatic Death

A sudden death is also regarded as a traumatic death, because it is one that is unexpected and often viewed as preventable. The grieving process with traumatic grief is intensified and frequently complex, for the surviving parents. Coping with a sudden death can be even more demanding than a normal grief as parents are left asking "Why?"

"No one should expect a surviving parent to return to normal, but everyone should expect over time that the surviving parent will, in the spirit of the child who has died, begin to live again, to be functional and to have purpose. This is the new normal." [1]

In the above referenced article Dr. Dyer mentioned the Compassionate Friends. This national organization was founded by Simon Stephens, providing a resource of support and compassion to any family who has had a child die from any cause. As founder he has stated: "**The Compassionate Friends** is about transforming the pain of grief into the elixir of hope. It takes people out of the isolation society imposes on the bereaved and lets them express their grief naturally. With the shedding of tears, healing comes. And the newly bereaved get to see people who have survived and are learning to live and love again". Compassionate Friends has grown over four decades to more than 625 chapters with locations in all 50 states, as well as Washington, DC and Puerto Rico.[2]

Blessed are those who mourn, for they shall be comforted. Matthew 5:4 NKJV

> *Saturday morning November 10th* - I get to see my baby today. She's with God now. There will be no more pain for her, no more suffering, and no more tears. 10:00 a.m. is the time set up to go see her. Doc, Lisa, mom, and I will be going to the funeral home. I am having her cremated and then take her home with me where she belongs. I invited Donna – Jimmy's mom to meet us there so she could say goodbye too.

According to Judge Robinson, who also is part owner of the funeral home, I have to get Jimmy's permission to have Becca cremated since he is next of kin. Tell me how dumb that is, he killed her and now he gets to say what can be done. If he refuses to agree then I have to get a lawyer and petition the court for me to handle the disposal of her body. He might as well agree because I'll spend what ever it takes to keep her home now.

There are two things I have planned to do when I get to the funeral home. One is I want to take a picture of my baby and then I just want hold her. Nobody else wants me to take pictures. They think it is wrong but I want to. What is so wrong with that, if it makes me feel better? I don't want to upset them now so I'll wait until the right time to take my picture and no one can prevent it then. Mom has decided she doesn't want to see Becca so she won't be going into the family room with us. She chose to walk around the parking lot while we were with Becca and she picked up a colored marble which she still carries in her purse.

There is my baby on that bed. She is totally wrapped to the top of and around her head, but she looks so peaceful. This is so unreal. She would like the fact she is bundled like a baby to stay warm – she was always so cold. When I read the belongings record the police had, the listing included six pair of socks - two brown and four white. Now tell me she didn't tend to get cold. They let me lean down next to her and hold her for awhile. I talked to her and let her know she was coming home to the serenity room with Elvis. I could see the smile when she heard that. You see I have collected Elvis memorabilia since I was four years old and no one (at least in my family) loves him like Becca and I do.

The time to leave came much too soon, but before I left they cut a lock of her hair for me to keep. There was still blood in it. I had a little blue velvet pouch that I placed her hair in, and now I carry that in my wallet. They explained that since she was to be cremated they didn't embalm the body so I had to be careful how I touched her. It is hard to walk away and know she will never come to my house again, never pick up the phone and say "I just needed to talk to my mommy", and never ask me to braid her hair for her, hold my hand as we walk down the street because she didn't care how old we were, the daisies that she would unexpectedly drop off at the office just to say she cared. You see, all that is left of these many things is my memory, like her favorite Elvis song "Memories" locked between the pages of my mind.

I talked to the kids today (at least Leslie, TJ isn't talking) and Leslie is going to come in for the celebration, so Doc will drive to Harriman, Tennessee, tomorrow to pick her up while Lisa and I are at church. Mom has decided to go to church with us instead of staying home alone. We will sit on the front pew, which is where Becca and I always sat.

> *Sunday November 11<u>th</u>* – Mom, Lisa and I went to church while Doc went to pick up Leslie, I'll take her this afternoon to tell her mom good bye. TJ isn't going to come. Sue said he is having a hard time coping right now. I would expect that, since the last time he saw his mom, was in a court room and he told her she wasn't his mother and he wished she were dead. At least that was Becca's perception of the meeting. You see Tim and Sue filed for full custody of the kids, with Sue actually adopting them. Becca truly believed that was what they wanted, but before she signed anything she wanted to see them one last time, and then she would make up her mind. She went to court in Johnson City and came back with the opinion they wanted nothing to ever do with her again so she signed the adoption papers September 11, 2007, her last act of love that involved the kids was to give to them the freedom from

her she thought they wanted. Therefore, if TJ had said to his mom he never wanted to see her again then it looks like he got his wish and now he will have to live with that, but he needs to be able to forgive himself. She would never want him to hurt because of her. I wish I could get him to talk to me so he would know how much she loved him and that she never meant to cause him any pain.

When we got to church, located on the front pew, where Becca and I always sit, was a single stem silk red rose for her. I will keep it with her in the serenity room. It lies under the chest with the rose bud in front of the opening. I keep thanking God that at least I got to talk to her the night she died. She had called me that afternoon during her break at work and we talked awhile just about things in general. She told me that she had told Jimmy she was going to leave and he asked her to give him until January to get himself straightened up and back on the right track. She said he cried and seemed to really want to be different so she agreed.

I think of all the times she would mention to me leaving and going to Rachel's or getting a place of her own. Why wasn't I hearing her need to get out and help her to do so, instead of telling her to make sure she had enough money saved to make the move and take care of herself? When we started to hang up she said "I know you would help mom, but I don't want to cause problems for you and Popi, I love you" "I just needed to talk to my mommy". Little did I know these were the last words I would hear her say?

I stop to think back about church that morning. I don't remember off the top of my head the scripture, but am sure I wrote it down because that is what I do every Sunday. What I do remember is Buddy making a statement to the affect that he knew Becca was in heaven and that she had told him many things he would never tell me. I thought at the time it was strange for him to say that and that someday I would confront him, but today wasn't the time.

Even though it was Sunday, Judge Robinson took the release for cremation papers to Jimmy at the jail to sign. By law he would have to read the papers to Jimmy (since Jimmy told him he couldn't read very well) and after explaining what they said, he would then have to answer any questions Jimmy might have. At first, he said, Jimmy was in agreement with what I wanted to do, and then he started asking questions as if he didn't understand. Judge Robinson said he wasn't comfortable with letting him agree to the cremation when Jimmy hesitated in giving permission and answered and asked questions as if he really wasn't sure what he was agreeing to.

According to Judge Robinson, Jimmy starting telling him a story about blacking out and not remembering what had happened, so guess that means mental evaluations will have to be done before court can proceed. I actually expected that to happen since Jimmy has a history of being bipolar and because of the brutality of the murder. No problem, whether a refusal or just not understanding, I won't let him win on this one. Tomorrow is a holiday (Veterans Day) so on Tuesday I will go to court to get the legal right to cremate Becca and take her home, and then have her Celebration of Life on Wednesday night at the church. Even though Leslie got here mid-afternoon we have to wait until tomorrow for Leslie to see her mom, so I AM GOING to take pictures then. It seems strange I can't just go to the funeral home and see her anytime I want.

There must be an employee of the funeral home in attendance when we see her, so tomorrow it is.

Monday November 12<u>th</u> – it's time to see my baby again before they take care of her for me. Leslie asked for a lock of her hair also, but I couldn't cut it this time, the care giver at the funeral home had to. It has been three days and starting a fourth so we have to be really careful with touching her. I got my picture. There is a small bruise on her eyelids, and a cut on her lip. Still she had that beautiful, peaceful look of being asleep on her face.

But I do not want, you to be ignorant, brethren, concerning those who have fallen asleep, lest you sorrow as others who have no hope. For if we believe that Jesus died and rose again, even so God will bring with Him those who sleep in Jesus. 1 Thessalonians 4: 13-14 NKJV

Tuesday November 13<u>th</u> – There are so many things to take care of, but first I have to know I can take possession of my baby legally. I went to the court house this morning to see the judge – Honorable David R. Kennedy, Judge of the Seventh Circuit Court of Davidson County, Tennessee. We did not have to actually have a hearing, but instead were seen in his chambers before his court actually started. It didn't take five minutes for him to read through the request and sign, giving me permission to have Becca cremated.

From the court house we went to the funeral home with the signed papers so they could proceed with the cremation.

Lana Spencer from the office came by today with enough groceries to last for a month or more. The office also took up a collection and it will be sent to the YWCA – Weaver Domestic Violence Center of Middle Tennessee. The shelter is the largest in the state with 58 beds for helping and providing a safe place for victims who are able to get free. In a few days, Doc and I will find the time to go there and volunteer to do whatever we can and to make sure they know that donations will be coming in Becca's memory.

In taking care of things today we had to go to the Lentz Public Health Department to get certified copies of the death certificate. When closing out any insurance claim there must be a certified copy of the death certificate sent to the insurance companies, as well as a copy of the police report and obituary from the local newspaper. Charles E. Shaw is the police officer who filed the report which lists the statement from Jimmy as saying he had blacked out, awakened to see his wife lying on the floor, and called mobile crisis. It's interesting that the report also indicates Jimmy's brother approached the officer when he arrived, which means Jimmy called Thomas (which is earlier described) before he called 911. The report indicates that Nashville Fire Department engine 35 was on the scene attempting to administer medical aid. Becca's date of birth is listed as April 24, 1974 which is incorrect, she was born in 1972. They had her age correct but not the year; would you not check your math on legal reports?

<u>*Wednesday November 14*</u> *-* We went to pick up Becca at the funeral home. I have to laugh for a moment. Becca was the type person who never saw a stranger. If you showed her kindness and she felt you needed it in return she was there for you. She had friends of all races, some gay some straight and loved them all, and was a friend to them when they needed her. When I went to get her ashes they handed her to me from a closet in a small designer paper bag (*Phillips-Robinson Funeral Home*). I slowly walked out to the car with my head lowered while walking and told Doc (my husband) we had a problem. You could see the concern on his face as he asked what. I looked up into his eyes and said "I hate to tell you this but Becca just came out of the closet". She would so have laughed and appreciated that. You see Doc has his own opinions as to lifestyle and culture. An opinion many agree with but as I stated Becca never saw a stranger and loved everyone that came into her life. Even those who didn't deserve the love she had to give.

And Jesus answered him, The first of all the commandments is, Hear, O Israel; The Lord our God is one Lord; And thou shalt love the Lord thy God with all thy heart and all thy soul, and all thy mind and all thy strength. This is the first commandment. And the second is like it, namely this, Thou shalt love thy neighbor as thyself. There is none other commandment greater than this. Mark 11: 29 – 31 NKJV

CHAPTER TWO

Celebration of Life

You are all invited to attend the Celebration of Life
for Rebecca Lynn Ollis-Coons.
Born April 24, 1972, Deceased November 09, 2007.
Dress is anything Eeyore.
Come prepared to share your stories.

*B*ecca's Celebration of Life was held tonight November 14, 2007, at the Eastwood Baptist Church. Death makes us let go of people, but life of a loved one gives reason to celebrate. So I decided to celebrate all my little girl had given to me, not mourn and question why, as many do. God will take each of us in His time, not ours, so I chose to celebrate the time I had been given by God to share with my daughter.

I was so utterly surprised at the turn out. There was standing room only. Family had come from North Carolina, East Tennessee, Arizona, and her half sister – Rachel, from Florida. I was so happy to see she had so many friends, from the school, from the neighborhood, and even from her work – current and past. She really had touched a lot of lives. A mother can be proud of that - I didn't realize she had touched so many lives. I also had support from my co-workers at the office where I work, those who worked with the both of us at the children's camp, and our church family.

The celebration was about family and friends talking about the time we had each shared with her. The music playing as all entered was "Elvis" for her and for me. You see that is something we always shared together – our love for the king of rock and roll. Each Christmas she would give me something with Elvis on it, a collector's hound dog animal, a box of candy, or an ornament that was her gift to me. I have been collecting memorabilia since I was four years old and Becca would have inherited my collection. At some point of time in the future, I have decided to sell most items from my collection and donate the money to domestic violence. Hopefully I can start a non-profit organization and raise monies for the cause, I will call it the INO Foundation – It's Not Okay, Domestic Violence.

Buddy Jarrell, the Pastor at Eastwood Baptist Church opened the celebration with prayer. I remembered in my head (as previously mentioned) that when I told him about Becca, he made a statement that he knew things they had talked about but he wouldn't share with me what had been going on. It seemed strange that if he had no intention of ever telling me anything that he would bring it up to begin with. I believe in the privacy of conversations between ministers and members being just that - private, but why clergy shouldn't be required to report to law enforcement the suspicions of abuse, the same as medical personnel are required, to do I don't understand. That alone might have made a difference. I have to tell myself everything happened as it did for a reason, but it doesn't mean I like it and want to try to make a change in some of our laws.

After a few moments of Buddy talking, I took over the ceremony and asked for friends or family to come forward and share with all of us what they had experienced with Becca in their life. Lisa – Becca's sister read first from Max Lucado's *Grace for the Moment,* a day by day inspirational reading book. Her choice was to read from the date of Becca's birth April 24th and the date of her death November 09th. The passage for the 24th was entitled "<u>Confession Creates Peace</u>", *Happy is the person whose sins are forgiven, whose wrongs are pardoned Psalm 32:1.* The reading from the 09th was entitled "<u>A Compassionate God</u>" and says: *He comforts us every time we have trouble, so when others have trouble, we can comfort them. 2 Corinthians 1:4.* Lisa also talked about them being little, times they shared as sisters. One particular time was them sitting together playing on the piano at their Nanny's house and pounding out the simple notes to a song recorded by the Righteous Brothers – **"He".**

He can turn the tide and calm the angry sea.
He alone decides who writes the symphonies.
He lights every star that makes the darkness bright.
He keeps watch all through each long and lonely night.
He still finds the time to hear a child's first prayer, saint or sinner call and always find him there, though it makes him sad to see the way we live
He always says I forgive.

Even at that young age the girls knew God and church and that when no one else was there, God was. In Becca's final moments I can only pray that God held her close and she felt His loving arms wrapped securely around her and not the pain inflicted by the knife Jimmy was using. That is the loving God I know and I truly know in my heart He was there with her. I also know that as the last line mentioned above from the song "He always says I forgive" that I too must forgive Jimmy. To allow God to help me make it day by day and not feel anger but forgiveness – I do not feel anger; I feel joy knowing my baby is at peace and free of pain, there is no hatred, just a peace because I do forgive.

Classmates from Draughn's Junior College came forward and shared the impact she had on their life, the classes they shared, the conversations related to their future. Sadly enough she had also shared some of the fear she had of Jimmy, and the things he had done to her. It was those thoughts she never really shared with me, but I am glad she did have someone to talk to. No matter how young or old we might be, it's important that we each have someone to talk to in times of need. Though we may pray to God for all our needs and concerns, we still need that human contact and trust in a person in time of conflict. That someone who we know will not criticize but listen, laugh with us, not at us, and cry alongside of us when we hurt.

Having just completed her degree in Criminal Justice in September, one classmate talked about them buying a CSI lab game from the local Kmart and racing to see who solved the crime first. Jenna said she never completed hers, but Becca did, and made it a point to call her and tell her it was solved. Another talked about the laughter she brought to others faces and the pranks she liked to pull. She was really close to Ms. Martha who became her safety net when Jimmy was on a tangent. The lady who she could call and go stay in a safe place where he couldn't find her. So many times it was Ms. Martha she turned to and I thank God she was there. You see she did tell me there were times when she and Jimmy got into an argument that she would go to Ms. Martha's, but she never told me about the physical abuse. Whenever I saw any bruising, she explained it away. I remember one time that she had bruising on her right arm and face, she told me that she had to work security for a teen RAVE and the kids got out of control. I never doubted her explanations. Should I have been more tuned in then, that it was more than just the security jobs she was working? I knew Jimmy had a temper. Why was I so wrapped up in my own life that I didn't see? What kind of mother was I not to see the pain my baby was suffering?

Members of our church family took a few moments to say a few words. I remember Terrell putting his arms around my shoulders and saying "You know Becca is in heaven and got to kiss Elvis before you did", how could I not have a smile come to my face. Ms. Reba our pianist sang a special song in Becca's memory. She chose a song written by James Stover and Michael Williams, made famous by the Kingsmen entitled "Wish You Were Here".

And *I know if you could talk to me now*
Here's what you'd say to me
Oh I wish you were here
It's such a beautiful place
Wish you were here
Nothing but clear sunny days
It never rains no one complains
We haven't seen a tear
We're having a great time
Wish you were here.

I really couldn't imagine her being gone, but I know she is and I must think of those good times and that I will see her again someday. It would probably be very uncomfortable for most people to comprehend what I had done, but I wanted everyone to know that Jimmy's family was present at the church. Becca had been a part of their family and I felt they deserved to tell her goodbye the same as her other friends.

Trying to say goodbye was not in my thought process. I wanted her remembered for always and forever, for being a daughter, a sister, a mother, and a friend. That is what a celebration is all about. Thanks to a friend in Kentucky who couldn't be present, the final song of the evening was "He" Jane had the song over nighted so it could be played just for Becca as a remembrance that "He" had her in his hands and His protection until we meet again.

I can't remember all the words of comfort that were said after the celebration, but I can see the faces of friends and family. I have pictures taken by a church member, so that will help me to go back and remember who all was there. Following the ceremony I took her to her earthly resting place in the serenity room at my residence in which my collection of Elvis is housed.

Take a minute to visualize her resting place; hanging above the pewter colored chest which contains her ashes is a shadow box that holds her security badge, to the right is the honorary degree in Legal Assisting – she was working on this degree at time of death, and to the left is her degree in Criminal Justice. As I positioned her degrees and knew how proud she was of the accomplishment, I thought briefly about how she would have processed the crime scene. Would her body have remained in the kitchen\dining room floor for over eight hours? Would I as the mother have been allowed to see her before they took her, or even see her at the morgue? What I remember now with peace in my heart is that God has her in her heavenly home where she is finally at peace; He'll take better care of her than I ever could. I thank Him for giving her to me for the time He did.

Maybe it was because I have placed my child where I can talk to her, keep her close, and know she will never be hurt again, that this night's sleep actually came easier than the past few. Is this the time I am supposed to start letting go? I don't think so. There are so many things to do now that I don't know where to start first. So where I must start is to say "good night my precious baby, I am here for you now". My routine will now begin to kiss her good night and tell her I love every day that my head lays on the pillow in the same house.

And God will wipe away every tear from their eyes, there
shall be no more death, nor sorrow, no crying. There shall
be no more pain, for the former things have passed away.
Revelation 21:4 NKJV

CHAPTER THREE

Time Keeps Passing

Everyone has gone home now. It's just me and Doc and Becca. You can't help but wonder what steps you are supposed to take next and where the strength will come from to take the first step and then each one that is to follow. I spent a few hours going through some of her belongings, trying to figure out if Leslie would want anything and knowing TJ wouldn't, at least not now, but maybe someday. I think one of the first things I am going to do is put together a "Memory Album" for the kids. There can be a section for when Becca and Tim met and married, one for each child and then one of the kids and Becca together. I would love for them to be able to look back at pictures and remember the good times shared with their mom.

I remember trying to figure out who I could talk to about Becca that really knew her. It was very obvious early on that I couldn't talk to TJ, Leslie and I did talk about her mom without hesitation, my mom seemed to be uncomfortable talking, Lisa talked some, but I didn't feel comfortable talking to Doc, my husband. You see he was fighting his own battles with not making peace with

Becca and I still searched my heart and mind as to the fact that had they not been at odds she might have been at my house and away from Jimmy. I remember her saying to me just a week before her death that she didn't know why 'Bubba' was mad at her, but that she would never ask for anything that might cause me to have any problems with him and that meant a place to stay. She talked about getting a place with Jenna from school or her going to live with Rachel – her half sister. She had at least started looking at moving on and making a better life - one without Jimmy and I know one without pain.

As I move forward now there is a need to get through, to get up each day and function knowing she is gone, knowing the phone will never ring again with her just saying hello. Guess that is what coping is all about. In trying to understand and deal with the day to day feelings, I researched many web sites for words of strength or guidance on how to cope. There were often common points to be considered stood out in my mind that are worth mentioning.

How I managed to Cope with Death

Remembering and honoring the person was top of the list. Becca had become such an understanding person and thinking of others as she fought her own battles that I had to think about how she might handle a crisis such as this. One thing I knew without hesitation is that she had planned a future helping others who were victims of Domestic Violence and now I had to step into her shoes and fulfill that role. Somehow I think she would expect that of me, to be sure she wasn't forgotten, and that what she had started was important and would be carried on.

As I look at my husband who tries to be strong and not shed a tear I can feel the guilt he carries now and know that I can't comfort him. Why the world ever thought a man shouldn't show emotions, but should be the strong one and not cry is crazy. Any person who feels like crying should cry you can't worry about what others think; maybe they are waiting to see if you can cry before they do.

As time moved on it seemed no one remembered or cared about my loss, it was back to the daily grind for them. I have learned now that a piece I was missing was someone who I could talk to and who would talk back about Becca. That is an important component of being able to deal, having that ear to listen and voice to share.

Special Days should be Remembered

I count the weeks since Becca's death instead of the month or year. You see to me she died a certain day of the week, not just a date in a given month or year. Calendar time changes since some months have four weeks and some have five, but Friday never changes.

I know the first year Thanksgiving, Christmas, her birthday, and Mothers Day were the hardest. You have to allow that pain to surface and work through it. Having something special to share with a connection to them is important, if you did something with them on those dates then still do it, take a friend or another family member in their place and the two of you remember the loved one together.

The dates on the calendar are tough. Birthdays, anniversaries, Christmas, they all hurt, especially the first time around.

Especially during the first year, find a way to make them (or their memory) part of those special days. Eat at their favorite restaurant, buy a gift for a family member in their honor, do something that sparks an old memory.

Healing takes Time

Physiologically everyone heals at a different rate in time so why would we think emotional healing is any different. Time heals all – or at least that is what they say. It may take a week, a month, or even years. That is okay. Keeping the loved one near you and honoring them will help. Becca will always be in my heart and if times are tough I know her love is there to help me get through.

At the strangest times in your life you may remember something they said or did and a smile will come to your face and you'll find yourself laughing. So allow that laugh – it is okay to laugh again. With the laughter the pain begins to subside and the laughter will bring joy of memories gone by.

My focus now is to get things in order and work with the District Attorney to assure Jimmy is tried for what he has done in a legal court of law. You see no matter what the court system does, the day will come that he still has to face God, the almighty judge. I must also realize that if while imprisoned he finds God, then God can and will in fact forgive him, and Jimmy too may also be in heaven for eternity. I had to take a deep breath with this thought, but that is exactly how our all forgiving and loving God works. No matter our sins, if we confess them to God and ask for forgiveness, we will be granted just that – Forgiveness.

Friday November 16th – I received a letter in the mail

today from Symetra Financial, an insurance company that handled coverage for Walden Security where Becca worked. Evidently she had taken out a $10,000 life insurance policy and made me beneficiary for 50% and Jimmy 50%. I never knew she had this and don't know if Jimmy did or not. Surely he will not benefit from killing her. One thing I am learning is to expect the unexpected. You think you know what goes on with your kids, and then you remember you barely kept up with them when they were young and under our roof. Once they are adults you never know what their day to day life is about. What you must hold onto is the hope you taught them a few things about life and living. This seems to be one time that Becca thought ahead and did a good thing, looking out for her future needs, by giving to someone else.

Monday November 26th – I decided that today was the time to sit down and write letters to the insurance companies, where I have coverage on both the girls and actually the grandkids also. There may be a problem with one policy because I can't remember who the beneficiaries are and one of my concerns is that the paperwork had been done for Sue to adopt the kids (October 25, 2007) and I'm not sure I want Tim to have control of their money. Doc actually talked to Tim about filing and getting social security for the kids from their mom's death benefits. Since it has only 15 days from the adoption papers being filed they may not have been finalized before Becca died, so the kids may be able to draw a monthly check from her until they turn 18. That should at least help toward their college education. Funny isn't it that they didn't want anything from her in life, but in death she will provide for them. When they are older, they will realize how much they were loved and that above everything else, she only wanted them to be happy. I remember her coming back from court and feeling like the kids hated her. It broke her heart to sign those papers, but she truly felt that was what they wanted. So what I must do is trust Tim to be the father he has always been and God to protect us all.

The eyes of the Lord are on the righteous, and His ears are open to their prayers.   I Peter 3:12 NKJV

<u>*Tuesday December 25th*</u> — Doc and I were supposed to have gone on a trip together this year, but I just couldn't be away from the grandkids this Christmas. I'm not sure he really understands, but he would never tell me no. Instead we drove to North Carolina to be with the other grandkids and Lisa. Joshua asked me during a phone call if Becca was coming too, so I took Becca with us to Lisa's house. Out of respect for Lisa, I did let her know my conversation with Joshua and made sure she was comfortable with Becca being there. The

other kids, according to Joshua, wanted her to be there for Christmas too. They hadn't gotten to come to the celebration because of school and not knowing how long their mom would be with me so they felt left out. They did get to see Becca when they came in for vacation in June. I have some really good pictures of them together and a picture of Lisa and Becca together, the first in a long time and the last. Lisa actually at some point, I don't remember exactly when, took that picture and gave it to me in a frame that says best mom. They both had a silly grin on their face, looking happy and care free.

After we got to the house and got suit cases in, Joshua asked if he could talk to Becca. I took his little hand, we walked over to the mantle where she was sitting and he just talked, about nothing of any great importance, but he said what he needed to say in his own little heart and mind. Keep in mind, he was only four years old and I'm sure didn't understand all that was going on, but did know his Aunt Becca was gone. Coming from a Christian home, he did know about God, heaven, and praying. His mom said he prayed for his Aunt Becca each night.

Becca loved Christmas and the trees, so this year before we left for North Carolina, I put up her "Charlie Brown" tree, the one she always had for TJ in his room. All the ornaments on the tree are ones Becca and the kids made together. It is lopsided with no true shape, but there is so much love hanging on the limbs you can almost feel it. I hung a small Eeyore just for her. That will be a new tradition in my house until TJ decides he wants the tree… if he ever does.

I haven't been able to get him to talk about his mom. If I mention her to him, he stops talking and once even hung up on me. Sue said one day she found him crying and he said he had been thinking of his mom, but he wouldn't talk about it. I hope that some day he will find someone he can confide in and get his feelings out. He seems so unhappy at times. No child should have that much pain in his life and if that pain comes from or because of his mom, then please God, help him to find forgiveness in his heart and to know how much she really loved him.

Behold children are a heritage from the Lord. The fruit of the women is a reward. Like arrows in the hand of a warrior. So are the children of one's youth. Psalm 127: 3 – 4 NKJV

<u>*Friday December 28th*</u> – We made an appearance in probate court today to file a small estate affidavit in Becca's name. You are supposed to list outstanding debts that are known and who the account is with. Unfortunately, I had no idea who she owed with the exception of a signed agreement she had with me so that is all I listed. Another requirement is to list her survivors and where they resided. I had no idea where her dad was and it was easy to list Jimmy's where about – local jail - and then to list the address of the kids.

2008 A New Year

Thursday January 9th – it's interesting how dates and days stay connected, the ninth of the month and a Thursday. They will never convince me that her death was on Friday. When Jimmy stabbed her late Thursday evening and left her that is when she really died not when 'people' got there to say so. The autopsy report came in the mail today. Took it long enough to get to us. I actually faxed the request with all my contact numbers to the Medical Examiner's office on November 20, 2007. They stamped the form as mailed on January 07, 2008. The report was a total of twelve pages long which included drug screening reports which indicated nothing in her system not even an aspirin. Suppose at some point I was concerned about that because I knew she had previously been taking pain pills for the back injury she sustained in the car accident.

Doc opened and read it first and was pretty upset; he couldn't even tell me about it. I am out of town again, and surprisingly enough I am again in Shelby. What are the chances of that happening again unless it was preplanned? I will have to wait until I get home to read the report myself.

Friday January 10th – arrived home without incidence and wanted to read the autopsy report. How can anyone tell you someone didn't suffer when they have 17 stab wounds and five defensive wounds? Then there was mention of abrasions on her knees. My first read through the autopsy of course was as a mother and very emotional and then I went back and read as a nurse and dissected the report. 22 total cuts don't sound to me like she didn't suffer. Why do people always say that, when if you didn't feel the violence, how could you know whether or not a person suffered? I just thank God she doesn't have to suffer anymore at the hands of Jimmy. She can rest peacefully and know mom will make a difference in someone else's life because of and for her. Her life will have meaning and somehow help many others through the work I plan to do for domestic violence, all in her memory.

What I find interesting is that the autopsy report states the time of death as 6:05 a.m. and the Medical Examiner was notified at 5:18 a.m. Another interesting statement is found in the police report, which lists the initial call at 00:58 hrs and report at 02:00 hrs. Now what takes five hours before death is listed by the Medical Examiner when there was EMT on the scene that could have pronounced? So, what time did she really die? There is also a note on autopsy report that L.V. Long was dispersed to the scene to examine the body and actually pronounced her death, but no time of his pronouncement is listed. The police report has an error in Becca's birth date, the report stated 1974 as year of birth when she was born 1972. There was a previous wife named Rebecca – could that have been her birth year?

Friday January 18^{*th*} *–* The mail today consisted of an insurance check from the company coverage where she worked. It was very strange to open the check that was insurance money she thought to leave for me. It shows the maturity she had developed and insight to know someone would need to see about her care if and when something happened. She had talked to others about her fear of Jimmy and this may be part of the reason she took out the policy, but why would she include him on the policy?

Because it was murder there was an accidental death benefit coverage clause so I received a check for $10,000 instead of the face value of $5,000. She found a way to pay her mom back even in death. I knew how responsible she had become, but I never dreamed of this. She had only been with the company for approximately 45 days so the policy had to have just been issued. Not sure what the court will do with the $10,000 Jimmy is supposed to get, but I do know I will fight against him ever getting anything.

Wednesday January 23rd – I received notification from court in the mail today that I could now legally act as Administrator of Becca's estate. Not exactly sure what all this means because fortunately it is a role I have never had to serve in before. I suppose this entails actually closing out all the accounts I have already taken care of, disposing of her personal property in any way I choose to do – again already done. There was no one to challenge what had been done, so I guess it was all okay.

<u>*Wednesday February 13*</u> – After talking with Tim several times and knowing he will look after the interest of the kids, the courts will be appointing him as Administrator of Becca's estate acting for the kids. This became active March 7, 2008, (also the date of the first court hearing). There was still an outstanding court hearing related to the auto accident she had in June 2006. It appears this will now be settled and the kids will be awarded the settlement. Also after several months, the one insurance policy that I had taken out when she was a teenager does have the kids listed as beneficiary, but since Becca owed me money Tim and I agreed as did the courts, that the life insurance policy would be divided between me and the two kids, it will be about $10,000 for each of us. Between the insurance she left me and now this, it is actually more than she owed…I would rather have her here, than the debt paid.

<u>*Friday March 7ᵗʰ*</u> – This morning becomes the first of many court hearings. The agenda for the first one is to determine if Jimmy is mentally competent to stand trial. From what I understand one of his first statements to officers was a claim that he blacked out and that he can't remember what happened, much less what he did.

When Doc and I arrived at the court house we met Heidi Bennett from the Metro Nashville Victims Assistance Support

Office and Susan Tucker from the DA's office. They talked to us before we went in the court room to prepare us as to what would be going on. Jimmy would be brought into the court, the judge would ask his attorney some questions, then the Detectives and officers who were at the scene would make statements about receiving the call and what they saw upon arrival. They prepared us that parts of the testimony might be descriptive, but that neither Jimmy, nor we would make any statements at this first hearing.

As I saw Jimmy come into the court room, I also noticed that he was totally alone. There was no one from his own family that showed up to support him. My heart actually went out to him. He was in the Metro orange jump suit with his hands cuffed in front of him. First the police officer who responded to the call testified and from my memory confused some of the times listed on the police report. Then Detective Shockley testified.

The bloody knife used to kill Becca had been found outside the apartment on the hill. No one knew if Jimmy took the knife out or someone else did. The first officer on the scene and the detective described what the room looked like, the location of Becca's body, and the blood on Jimmy. After the detective and officer finished talking, we all walked out into the hallway and talked for a few minutes. I gave Detective Shockley a picture of Becca to put in the files so they could see her for the beautiful, vibrant person she was, not the person at the scene they had pictured in their mind. The one I chose was of her in her cowboy hat, like the one I wear everyday on my left chest and the one in the serenity room. She would have made a great cowgirl, she sure looked the role, and loved country music. One of her most excited experiences was talking about the country stars she got to meet while serving in security with Rock Solid.

Now we have to wait for the grand jury to convene, which will not be until May. Believe me, nothing moves in the real world like it does on TV programs. Susan, from the DA's office, let us know it often takes a minimum of two years to get thru court hearings before the actual trial ever begins. Patience will now become a main part of my daily existence.

Thursday March 20<u>th</u> – I went to the Middle Tennessee YWCA this morning and filmed a public service announcement for them that will also be on DVD that they can share with others. My message is of course from a mother of a victim who had suspicions, but no proof of what was going on. Prior DVD's they had done were actual victims themselves talking of their experiences. I tried to stress the importance of needing to know what the signs of domestic violence are and what to do if you or someone you know needs help. The resources that are available are often unknown to many. We need to make the world aware of the signs and the fact that domestic violence is not acceptable. The YWCA will use the DVD for fund raising, meetings, and a public awareness message. It is called simply "Glenda's Story".

Friday March 21<u>st</u> – Today is Good Friday on the calendar. I received a phone call from Susan Tucker notifying us that the grand jury would in fact convene in May - another two months. At that time, they will decide if there is even going to be a trial- as if there was any doubt in our minds. Guess no one else really has any buy in or ownership to the situation – except of course, the police. She also talked about the local Victim Awareness Meeting\Dinner that is held in April of each year and invited both Doc and I to be a part of it. Another community awareness project that takes place, is the displaying of pictures of all the persons killed in and around Nashville. This takes place at the downtown main library from Friday April 11th – April 21st. I have the opportunity to send them a picture of Becca for display, and Doc will go to the meeting, while I am out of town. Seems like this year I am gone for all the important events and Doc has to stand in. This is bringing him front and center with Becca and having to deal with his own feelings, which he has never discussed with me.

Sunday April 20th – Doc and I went to the library today to see the pictures on display. One of the things he brought back to me from the meeting was a button they had made with Becca's picture. I will wear it every day. It is unbelievable to see all the young people who have pictures on display. Some are murders, some auto accidents, and some robberies gone wrong. They all look so 'normal'. Why do lives have to be taken this way? We all think we are going to grow to a ripe old age, but guess what, we just don't know.

Thursday April 24th — Today is a Thursday, Becca's first birthday after her murder and actually the day she was stabbed, even though they didn't call the police until after midnight and pronounce her death, until after 1a.m. She was stabbed on a Thursday. I can't call her and sing to her, or take her to dinner like I usually do, but I will spend time with her; does she know how much I miss her? I worry that tears aren't there often enough, that people think I am too strong and that they perceive me as not caring. If they only knew how my heart breaks every day. I try to keep my tears for the shower or for when I am alone because, I don't want Doc to see them.

Friday May 9th — *six months after Becca's death* — Tonight is Becca's graduation. There were rehearsals through out the day. Lisa came in to be here for me and for her sister. She also graduates tomorrow from a Masters Program in Education. She has worked so hard and I am so very proud of both my daughters. For Lisa to give up her graduation for her sister, shows how much she loved her, even when she didn't know the depth of the love she carried. She is showing that now.

Wearing Becca's cap and gown that she had pre-ordered made me feel so close to her. The entire class wore gold ribbons in her honor and remembrance. As we walked into the auditorium, I sat on the stage with the Director of the College and the Professors. I was honored to be one of the speakers at the graduation. Becca had touched so many lives at the school and many came up to me and talked about how she helped to save them from an abusive situation. I hope my message to this class of not accepting abuse reaches many, many, more and that they may avoid a death like Becca suffered. That they know there are people there to help them…they just have to reach out and speak out, asking for help.

Excerpt from my speech:

My purpose tonight is not to explain the signs to look
for, but to make you
aware that as you go out into the world with a
new sense of adventure, and a
new found purpose which you have been handed
today, that you keep your
eyes open to what is happening around you.

Love with a passion as you are meant to love, forgive
others as God has forgiven
all of us for things done in our life, but know there
are things that are not okay
and when they aren't, find the courage from within
to stop them.

If you are in an abusive situation – you don't have
to be – get help. Apologies
from abusers are only good for the moment, but that
is all it is, a moment or
two - it doesn't stop the abuse. No matter how badly
you might want that
*other person to change, **you** can't change them. All*
you can do is take a
stand to not let the abuse continue to happen to you
or to your friends or
family.

Talk to each other, talk to your professors, talk to
law enforcement, and talk
to sponsors of Domestic Violence Shelters and
STOP this vicious cycle of
abuse and death in our communities.

So as you move forward now from this special day,
know that what you
have accomplished is exciting, it's new and it
allows you the opportunity
to create something great. Life holds many
challenges for you. Be bold, be
adventurous, and be safe.

God Bless each and every one of you!!

After all the speeches and individual awards were completed, the degree presentation began. First, to a standing ovation, I accepted Becca's Criminal Justice Degree, Ms. Martha, her dearest friend, was at my side. Then with the Legal Assisting Class, I accepted for Becca, an Honorary Degree for a program she was enrolled in but would never be able to complete. Again, Ms. Martha was at my side.

Sunday May 11th - Lisa had to go home yesterday to be with her kids. It is Mothers Day and that is where she should be but I would have loved to keep her here. On Mother's Day last year, Becca faced her first year with Leslie being at her dad's and now this year I face them both being gone. It's almost as if I have lost everything that gave me strength to wake up. I know that isn't true, but how do you explain the pain that doesn't go away? I'll miss the single daisy she always gave me. She knew they were my favorites and made sure she got me one with a homemade card, one from her heart. So as I pull out the cards from years past, I remember my beautiful daughters and the joy each has brought to my life. I don't think any mother could be prouder of her kids, and I just hope they share that love and pride with them while they can. They grow up so fast and start lives of their own.

Friday May 23rd - What is it with all these Thursdays and Fridays? Susan Tucker called tonight and the Grand Jury did convene and indicted Jimmy on First Degree Premeditated Murder. The first court date is set for June 5th (a Thursday) in which the attorneys will exchange information. Jimmy will not be in the court room and Susan said we don't need to attend, but by all means could at anytime we wanted to. We talked about the possibility of Jimmy pleading guilty at some point and saving everyone a lot of time of going to trial; don't see that happening, but it sure would be nice.

I do not look forward to hearing all the details, but I want justice for Becca and I want her things back. The police report listed eight pair of socks as part of her possessions. I had to laugh because she always had the coldest feet, so to me that made sense for her to have that many pair of socks on; plus she had very narrow feet with wide work boots and needed support to wear them.

Thursday June 5th - Today is the first hearing between the attorneys. We'll await word from Susan as to what went on. The kidney camp starts this week, so I have to go set up before a patient and the state comes for survey and then the kids come Saturday. Becca was always a part of helping with the setting up the unit and decorating for the kids. Then she made the flowers and sash for the prom queen, and my costumes to wear for the week based on the camp theme. I have been a damsel in distress, a sixties hippie, a clown, and a Dallas Cowboys cheerleader. What fun times we had! I'm not sure how I'll get through this year but I will. I just have to remember how much it meant for us to do this together.

Monday June 9th — No word from Susan, so since I am at camp, I will be sending an email to find out what went on. I finally received a response late this afternoon and there was really nothing spectacular according to Susan. The attorneys shared information and set the next court date on August 7th – a Thursday. Susan says that will be sharing of further information and then hopefully the dates will be set for the actual trial to start. I would love to be a fly on the wall to hear if attorneys really banter like on TV when the attorneys make deals for a person's life.

At the kidney camp I volunteer at each year, I usually crown the king and queen at prom and Becca would come out for the dance. When her kids were home she brought them too and we all had a wonderful evening, dancing and celebrating. So many of the chronically ill kids will never see a prom at their own school, much less have the chance to be a prom king or queen. To see the joy in their eyes and laughter in their smile gives new purpose to life.

One of the nurses from Arizona who knew Becca, wanted to give an award in her name during awards ceremonies tonight. Others didn't want it to happen. They said it was not meant to be a memorial service and the award (charm) could go to me but it wouldn't be mentioned in front of the kids. That upset me to no end because Becca had been a part of the camp for five years and in my opinion, they wanted her to be ignored in the eyes of the campers who knew her and loved her. Maybe my judgment statement is a little steep, but it really hurt so I didn't go to the prom, I let them handle it themselves. Dennis, one of her dear friends, came to the dialysis unit at the camp where I roomed and we talked and cried about her. Then he went to the dance and I went to bed.

Monday June 16th — Lisa and the kids are here this week for vacation. Leslie came in with them. We were sitting on the back deck and Joshua walked up to me and said "Bepi, what did Jimmy to do Aunt Becca?"

I told him he stabbed her with a knife. He said "that wasn't very nice of him" then he asked if we could go in and talk to her. We went to the serenity room and sat in the rocker and looked at Becca's picture on the wall and talked to her for a while. He told her he loved her and missed her and wished Jimmy hadn't hurt her. It amazes me that kids feel much more than we realize at times and yet the simplest of explanations satisfies them. You see, you have to be open to share their thoughts or curiosity at any given moment and not lose a single opportunity that is opened to you. Once that time has passed, it's gone forever.

Monday July 07th — Today is my birthday. Another one of those "firsts" you have to face without your loved one. I found some cards she had given me in prior years – she always made homemade cards. Guess I'll have to keep them and read them every year now. The days still bring about my reaching for the phone to call her, even though I know she is gone, so I just go in her room and kiss her and sit in the rocker and talk to her. Some may think it is time to let go, but everyone has to do that in their own time, in their own way. I think any professional would say that to you, as long as it isn't interfering with your ability to function in daily life.

51

Sunday August 3rd — I got a phone call from both Jenna and Barbara Holman from Draughn's Junior College today letting me know that Ms. Martha had a heart attack in her sleep and died. She was at a family reunion in Maryland and her family went in to wake her up and found her. She was to have been a witness against Jimmy. As I reread this sentence it sounds selfish, but is really not meant that way. She and Becca had become very close at school, even though she was a student at age 60; this woman had a way with the students and loved them all. She was also an employee of the school who kept an eye open for unusual circumstances that were not supposed to be happening.

When Becca got into a fight with Jimmy and he became abusive, Martha is who she turned to. I am glad she had someone, but it hurts that she didn't come to me. I guess even after time has passed, I still wanted to be a better mom and am not sure why I wasn't. Maybe she would be alive if she had felt better about me as a mom, and I could have gotten her out of there. Yet, when I use my sensible mind, I know they say victims of abuse don't tell their loved ones because generally, the abuser threatens to hurt family. So in reality she was probably trying to protect me from any harm. Daughter looking after mom, I like knowing she cared that much.

The what if's remain even now and I know that someday they will disappear and if I take the time to be honest, there were times she tried to talk to me but she felt in her heart that because of the way she perceived Bubba felt about her, she didn't feel she could ask for help or a place to stay. I know I can't second guess things now because it happened for a reason and God had a reason, so I have to accept and go forward. Bubba truly has had some rough times handling his own demons and carrying his own guilt. It does no good to feel anger toward someone who is hurting themselves for their own reasons. What I have to do is forgive and know someday, he too will find peace within himself.

And the Lord, He is the One who goes before you. He will be with you. He will not leave you nor forsake you, do not fear nor be dismayed.   *Deuteronomy 7:6 NKJV*

CHAPTER FOUR

Will It Ever End

*T*hese days seem to go so slowly. I go into the serenity room each morning and every evening and kiss Becca and tell her to have a good day or to sleep peacefully. That is the beginning and the end of my day when I am not on the road traveling. I have been known to take her with me when I drive to a clinic that does not require flights. She never really got to travel during her short life, so I enjoy her being with me and sharing my trips.

Thursday August 7th – There was a second hearing with the attorneys today and I didn't want to wait to hear from Susan, so I called her. She states the trial date has been set for the week of March 2nd, 2009, still seven months away. Then she proceeded to tell me the city\ county didn't have any more money for jury trials until after the first of the year. She said that the trial should be over by Thursday of that week. We are actually going to trial before the usual two to three years waiting, so I am thankful for that.

I asked her about whether or not anyone had talked with Martha as a witness and told her what had happened. It is good to finally have a date, but the time seems so far off. You hear about the charged having the right to a speedy trial, well, why doesn't the victim have the same right? The family has to deal with all the waiting, the postponements, the disappointments, and all those unexpected things you never think about having to handle.

One of the unexpected I talk about, came in the form of a call today from Emily Plotkin, an attorney for Symetra Insurance Company. The insurance company is filing a suit to petition the court to handle the remaining monies from Becca's life insurance policy. It isn't that they don't want to pay they just don't want to say who the money goes to nor have to hold the monies until trial is over. Both I and Jimmy have to file a response with the court that says we agree to allow Symetra the ability to deposit the money with the court and then allow the court to disperse, when they choose to. It is okay with me to wait and see where the monies go, whether me, the kids, but surely not Jimmy. It's just another one of those hurry up and wait to see issues you never expect, something else to have to wait to settle, and something else that needs closure. You know most moms can wait a long time to do things for their kids and I can wait out the best of them.

> *Monday August 11<u>th</u> —* Actual court papers were 'served' on me at the office related to the insurance policy. I will have Doc read them also and we will come up with a response, file with the court, and plan to appear on Monday October 6th. These papers totally deal with the insurance company placing the monies still due

in the courts for dispersal, thereby removing them self from any decisions. One step at a time, it will all come together when it is meant to.

Thursday September 4ᵗʰ – Isn't it interesting another Thursday rolls around and I get a call from the DA's office. Susan states that Jimmy's lawyer has filed a petition with the court and we must now appear in court on October 15ᵗʰ at 1 p.m. The attorney is asking the court to suppress Jimmy's confession. I talked with Susan about the fact that Thursday seemed to be the 'information' days for news.

Just notified that on October 18ᵗʰ at 10 a.m. Nashville has an annual Domestic Violence Victims Awareness Celebration and roses are tossed into the Cumberland River in memory of all persons murdered during the year. I have to be at a corporate meeting in Florida and will miss out again, but Doc will be there for me and most important for Becca. It seems I miss everything that has to do with domestic violence right now when I need to be doing this for her. Is this how Doc is being forced to deal with his feelings by having to attend and represent us for Becca?

Monday September 7ᵗʰ – We went to the courthouse and filed the papers for the insurance company. At least that is done now. There are more processes and steps than I ever would have thought possible. The appearance is still scheduled for October.

Tuesday September 8<u>th</u> — Emily Plotkin called from the insurance company to let me know the court notified them that the response had been filed. She also stated that Jimmy had not responded and that by default the courts might automatically award me the money. I will just wait and see and whatever needs to happen, God will handle. What the shame is, is that this is blood money from the loss of my baby. Why couldn't I just have her back and forget all the money in the world?

Monday October 6<u>th</u> - I appeared in court in regards to the insurance company and no one else was there. I explained to the courts about Jimmy still awaiting trial and they asked me to inform them when the trial and sentencing was over and a decision would be made at that time, which is in my opinion the right thing to do.

Tuesday October 7<u>th</u> — Guess another court hearing brings back thoughts of everything that has happened. I was thinking about the EMT that took the time to talk to me that night when Thomas called. I decided to write a letter to his Captain because they wouldn't give me his name. Didn't matter that it had been almost a year, I still wanted him to know he crossed my mind. I mailed it to Captain David White and asked him to tell his EMT how much I appreciated what he had done in trying to save my baby, that he would never be forgotten in my heart or in the eyes of God. I wanted him to know that if I was able, I would give him a hug and thank him for being there since I couldn't be. I couldn't help but wonder what the thoughts were going thru his mind when he walks into scenes such as this one and know it must take a toll after awhile. Accidents and murder have to cause a different impact than do natural death calls. May God Bless our EMT's and civil servants for all they do.

Wednesday October 15th – Today is the first of many court appearances. My stomach is in knots. Not sure why – is it seeing him, is it even the remotest of possibilities that the court would throw out the confession, is it just that it is all still hanging over our heads? I have meetings at work all day today, but will leave long enough to go to the hearing. I will have some words for you tonight.

Doc and I went to court as planned. We spoke with Susan and Detective Shotwell before we went into the court room. Susan said that Jimmy's lawyer had decided to withdraw his petition to have the confession suppressed. So there may not be anything happen today after all. Is this the time of testing patience and strength and worry, then nothing happen? Susan did tell us that Katie told her when listening to the 911 call, that you could hear Thomas in the background saying "now Jimmy which knife was it you used?" That in itself is evidence enough not to allow suppression of the confession. We listened to the Judge question a couple of other attorneys regarding timeliness of filing petitions, then Mr.

Kalvecci actually withdrew Jimmy's petition so we were free to leave.

> *Saturday October 18th* — The Metro Davidson County Police Department along with the District Attorneys Office held a Domestic Violence Memorial Service today at 10:00 am at the Shelby Avenue Bridge. Interesting, Shelby Bridge and I was in Shelby when I got word, just a fleeting thought - those happen sometimes. I had to be at a corporate meeting which was out of state, so Doc went to support Becca. After the ceremony I spoke with him and he let me know how it went. He said there were eight victims of domestic violence who did not survive the attack during the calendar year of October 2007 thru October 2008.

Becca's name was the first called, then family members of the other seven also were presented with a rose and each persons rose was tossed into the Cumberland River as a Memorial to them. Doc, being the first to place a rose in the river, had his picture taken and was on the evening news, as well as, on the news stations website. We were able to go online and download a picture so Lisa and the kids saw it also. There were also awards given. Both Judge Robinson and Susan Tucker were presented with awards for the time and leadership they had been involved in, for the Victims' Services. The organization is actually called the Nashville Coalition Against Domestic Violence.

> *Saturday November 1st* — Talked with Lisa today and she plans to be here in March. She said this was the first

time in a year she had been able to let go of the anger for God not being there for Becca. I didn't even know she was feeling anger, guess because she is a Christian as am I, which I thought she was feeling the same things I was that God had protected Becca, not just taken her. Again, I so wish she had talked to me. Guess one of the realities of being a parent, is that your kids use other sources as their support system.

Friday November 7th — Today is 52 weeks or 364 days since Becca was pronounced dead. Some may say one year is the calendar date, but to me, I have counted the weeks. I have asked permission to light a candle for her at church Sunday and asked Ms. Reba to sing 'Wish You Were Here" the same song she sang at Becca's celebration of life. It is next to impossible to believe a year has passed and yet it seems so long to wait until March and a trial date. I was driving back from Albany, Georgia today, and with it being the anniversary and being alone in the car, all I could do was cry. Don't feel I need to burden anyone else with my feelings, so I try not to cry around anybody else. I found a good place was in the shower, no one knows but you and if you don't get too loud, they can't hear you over the running water.

Sunday November 9th - Today is the one calendar year anniversary. Everything was unusually calm today, being in God's house, knowing Becca was in the true house of God and that one day I would see her again, teaching Sunday school to the kids, Doc being here – meaning actually in church with me. God is the one who gets me through each day and I have to take His lead, I sure can't make it alone. Mom called but she didn't mention the date. Lisa had told me she was going to introduce Becca to her church, the first time she had really been able to talk about her sister. She carried the t-shirt with Becca's picture (I wore mine all day) and testified as to what her feelings had been for the past year and how she had finally gotten passed the anger. Wish I could have been there for her, so she knew how much I cared, and that her sister cared too. I never want to have to look back again and wonder if I was there enough for her, since I was never sure about being there for Becca or for either of them as kids.

Thursday November 27<u>th</u> – This is the second Thanksgiving without Becca. At church the preacher asked everyone to voice what they were thankful for. It's amazing the first thing that came to mind was being thankful that God had taken the pain and suffering away from Becca in His actually taking her. I knew she was at peace and by knowing that in my heart, then I can also be at peace. Doc and I spent a quiet day at home and then for dinner went to Ms. Reba's for a meal. In previous years, I would have gone to Becca's on Sunday before Thanksgiving for dinner with her and Jimmy and then we would have gone to North Carolina for the holiday. This year, we just stayed put.

Thursday December 4ᵗʰ - Here starts our Thursday patterns again. Remember I have always felt she actually died on Thursday even though she wasn't pronounced until Friday. Tonight is the Tennessee state Recognition Ceremony for Victims. Susan Tucker invited me to attend the ceremony at the capitol building tonight and to hang an ornament in the memory of Becca. Governor Phil Bredesen and his wife Andre Conte are the hosts.

Thursday December 11ᵗʰ - Tonight is the Nashville area homicide victims ceremony at Centennial Park. Doc met me at the office and we drove to the park together. It is really cold out – around 24 degree- but we both want to be there. This will be our first year participating, but I am sure not the last. Wanted to go last year but everything was just too fresh. It seems like March is such a long way off. There will be closure after all this is over with. There were so many families here – that in itself is sad, that people have to die so recklessly at the hands of others and not from the natural death God intended.

CHAPTER FIVE

When you're Alone

*I*t seems that day to day life keeps you busy just doing what needs to be done. Whether it is at home or work, you can generally keep your mind occupied. The nonsense things that you do just to get by never go away, the decisions you make may change but life in general, is still life. The holidays were very different this year. For the first time Doc and I went away for the season. First time I have ever been without the grandkids for Christmas. We needed some time but it was very hard. There is nothing going on with the courts right now, so I no longer had an excuse not to spend time with just him.

I have to say it was probably one of the best things I could have done. My ambitions in life had been to see Elvis in concert – did that twice – and to go to Hawaii. That is where our trip took us to the island of Maui. My highlight was snorkeling in the bay where Elvis snorkeled during the filming of Blue Hawaii – what more could a girl ask for.

2009 Another New Year

<u>*Wednesday January 28ᵗʰ*</u> — Got a phone call from Susan Tucker at the DA's office. There will be a pre-trial hearing on Wednesday the 11ᵗʰ of February. This is when the judge will hear from witnesses for the prosecution to determine if there is adequate information for the premeditation component of the charges. I will try to get a note to the school, so they can get in touch with the people there and have them get in touch with Susan. She asked me to document any information I might have seen or heard and include approximate dates.

<u>*Wednesday February 4ᵗʰ*</u> — I have had a really rough couple of days. I keep thinking about what Susan asked about information I might have and am so struggling. I know of verbal fights, one when I even got between them and probably stopped hitting from occurring (at least in my presence), but I can't with a clear conscious say I actually heard him say he would kill her. I vaguely remember him saying if he didn't have her, he would see to it that no one else would either, but is that what I really heard or, because of what he did, do I want to believe I heard it? There has been so much time pass, I want to help my baby, but I am really having a hard time with this, knowing what is right and wrong, not wanting to fabricate just for the sake of saying something, but not wanting to let Becca down. Please God, help me get through next week, then the trial next month.

<u>*Wednesday February 11*^{*th*}</u> _–_ There were six of us that testified before the judge for the purpose of determining who could actually testify in court and who wouldn't. Jimmy was in court, as was expected. I testified first and had to identify him as my son-in-law. Then I testified to what I had seen and heard transpire between the two, and actions\behaviors Jimmy exhibited in what appeared to be normal days and times of stress.

It was hard to listen to the others talk about what they saw and heard, Jenna and Lisa from school, Ms. Delvechio, one of Becca's professors, and one of the security guards, who had actually ran Jimmy off school property before. I just keep wondering why no one called and let me know. Probably because she was an adult and they don't report to moms, even when we think we should know what goes on with our kids regardless of age.

Staci Turner from the Medical Examiner's office testified. She explained there were 22 sharp force injuries.17 stab wounds, five incised wounds. Injuries included perforations to the heart, and the right and left lung. Wounds were located on her left upper back, total of six, ranging one to two, three quarter inches; right back, had one wound, one and half inches, which punctured the right lung. The left chest had a cluster of seven stabs, one inch to two three quarter inches, which punctured the heart and left lung. Jimmy didn't stop there; the right lower chest and abdomen also had puncture wounds, the examiner described. Then she described what could be perceived as Becca on her knees, trying to get away and holding her hands up to prevent being struck in the face. No one but Jimmy knows which stabs were first, but it does appear she tried to get away from him, so she couldn't have died instantly like the report tried to say early on. "My precious baby, no more pain".

Jimmy's attorney kept saying no one actually heard him say the word "kill" or saw him beat Becca. The judge read back a couple of statements and pretty much told the attorney to get real. It appears that we will all testify. Jury selection starts at 9am on Monday the 2nd of March, with trial starting as soon as selection is done. Hoping it will be over by Wednesday with a conviction of 1st degree murder, which carries a life sentence (which in Tennessee is 51 years) with no possibility of parole- he would have to serve the full 51 years. If the jury doesn't find him guilty and it goes to sentencing for a lesser charge (2nd degree), then the possibility is 15 – 25 years and he would be considered eligible for parole, based on good behavior. So now that this day is over, we wait for the trial in just under two weeks.

> *Friday February 27* – Got an unexpected phone call today, first from my husband, then from the DA's office. It seems that Jimmy wants to plead to second degree murder. This would carry a sentence of 15 – 25 and we could petition the court for the maximum which the court could set at 40 years. Katie (DA) was concerned that if we went to trial and even one person couldn't agree, then the lesser charge of second degree would be granted with a possible lesser sentence. As it stands, he had to admit his guilt and then know that the maximum he may face is 40 years with the least 15. Katie explained that with being able to bring his prior

convictions into play and the judge still hearing from the medical examiner and anyone else who wanted to make a statement, they feel sure he will get the maximum.

Jimmy must serve 85% of the 40 years before he would even be considered for parole and then there is no guarantee it would be granted, which would put him at about 72 years old. After long discussions with Susan and Katie and thoughts running through my head and my heart telling me I didn't want to subject Lisa or Bubba, or friends to hearing the descriptions again, I decided to accept the plea, which now means there will be a sentencing hearing on the 22nd of April. We will write letters now to the parole board since we may not be alive when and if he goes before the board for early release and our letters will still then be considered each and every time he became eligible, if he didn't get it the first time. Today, the people who wanted to say something were allowed to testify and then be cross examined by Jimmy's attorney. Lisa and Jenna were there from the school, as was Professor Delvechio. I was also put on the witness stand and allowed to voice my opinion as to what I thought the sentencing should be - can you guess what that was?

> *Tuesday April 14th* – Received a letter today from the pre-sentencing investigator giving me an opportunity to write letters for review prior to sentencing taking place. It was an opportunity to explain physical, mental, and financial impact on the family since Becca's murder.

<u>*Wednesday April 22*</u> – Today was supposed to be the sentencing. As we gathered to go into the court room, Ms. Alma and Ms. Faye from the church were there for support. Both knowing Jimmy and Becca, wanted to be there for us. As luck would have it, the paper work from the plea hearing was not completed and submitted for Jimmy and his attorney, so they tried to have it postponed. The judge decided since people were there to testify, she would still hear their testimony so they didn't have to miss more time from work or family. The first to testify, again, was me. Then it was the coroner.

It was difficult to sit and listen again as the coroner explained the stab wounds. There were a total of 22, five of which were defensive wounds on her hands when she shielded her face. Then again, the physical evidence that she had abrasions to her knees where it appeared she had tried to crawl away from Jimmy. You can't help but wonder what was going thru her mind at that time; you know there had to be fear for her life. Did she think of the kids, did she cry out to God to help her, or how fast was it all over?

The judge also accepted letters from Leslie (Becca's daughter) and Jeannie (Becca's aunt) into evidence, but the sentencing itself now won't be until May 26th a delay again. Maybe soon it will all be behind us and at least this part will be over and some semblance of normal life can begin.

Detective Shockley was there but did not have to testify this time. He did provide to us a form authorizing us to pick up Becca's belongings from the property room at East precinct. We went to the property room and got Becca's jewelry and phone. I didn't go through anything until we got home. I was okay until I held her phone in my hands. Lisa just held me and told me it was okay to cry, I must have sobbed really loud because it scared Doc and he came running down the steps to see what was wrong. Touching one of the last things she had touched, and for her blood to still be present, slapped me in the face with the reality of what not only had happened, but the fact that it was the last of her things I would come into contact with. The last thing she had in her possession before she died, probably trying to get help that never came.

<u>*Monday May 26th*</u> – Today we will finally know what lady justice actually does. It is hard to think this is almost over. For the first time, Jimmy's mom and Marie, his niece, are in the court room. Katie called me to the stand one last time. She asked a few questions very similar to all the others and then asked me what I felt should be done, my chance to really let everyone know I had forgiven Jimmy. However, I had been warned not to go down that road. I didn't want to be viewed as wanting to be easy on him. I told the judge I wanted Jimmy to receive the maximum she could give. That even with forty years he still had the opportunity to see people, to talk with his family. That Becca could never be the person she wanted to be – to help victims of domestic violence instead of becoming a victim. That her daughter would never have her mother at her graduation or wedding, nor

would I be able to hold her hand, or hear those last words my baby had said to me "I just wanted to talk to my mommie".

The judge then began reviewing all evidence given at the prior hearings and also reviewed Jimmy's history of arrest and violence. She was very careful to read each and every count Jimmy had ever had against him and the violence of those accounts, so they would be entered into court records. Jimmy had to again, aliquot to his actions and respond to understanding his sentence. It seems strange to me that he never visibly appeared to be regretful of his actions. He pretty much kept his head lowered and his eyes diverted, as to not look at me or the judge, but appeared to be looking into emptiness. His hair had grayed tremendously over this period of time, he had lost weight, his color was ashen, and this had to be hard for his mom to see. His attorney asked the court for consideration to be given and asked for a sentence of only 25 years. The judge explained that she was giving him the maximum, because of the violence of the murder and also his long history of arrest and violence.

So that was it, supposedly over with a 40 year sentence 85% of which had to be served before eligible for parole.

We gathered in the back room of the court and briefly talked with Susan and Katie before actually leaving the court room. What was going on in my head, what was I thinking, how was I feeling? Once we walked into the hallway, Marie grabbed my hand and asked me why I wanted Jimmy gone for so many years, that he loved Becca. I took a deep breath and tried to remain very calm. Looking her in the face I said "if he loved her he wouldn't have killed her". It was obvious Marie was upset as would be expected, but she yelled at me and said it wasn't fair for him to be gone for so long. Again, I calmly voiced to her that at least they could still talk to him, could visit him, but that I would never hear Becca's voice, see her, or hold her in my arms again.

Slowly my family and I walked away from the court for the last time. I restrained from turning and looking back one last time, whether to see reaction of Jimmy's family or to close a door that should never have been opened. My mind keeps thinking it's over – why don't I feel relief, where is the peace that should have come? Yet, this whole time, it was something for me to focus on, now I have to face the fact she is really gone. Now I have to call everyone and tell them the verdict, everyone has to let it go and move on. Please God, don't let them forget, don't ever think it is over, because she will never be over, she was a part of this earth, a part of life, a part of me, and a part of her children.

Tuesday May 27th – Just because the trial has closed, doesn't mean all things are closed. Little things keep appearing like this insurance issue, copies of the trial conviction have to be submitted to another court so final disposition can be made on the insurance monies in holding. It is my responsibility as family to assure this happens, so today I make that happen.

Tuesday July 14th – Received information today after inquiring, as to where Jimmy will be housed. Doc and

I requested to be listed on notification records so that anytime Jimmy is moved or when he becomes eligible for parole, I will be notified. Just to make sure letters are written and we as a family can respond to hopefully prevent his parole. Maybe he will then have to serve all forty years. There is actually even a website we can check for activity of his moves or behavior.

2010 A New Decade

Tuesday January 5th 2010 – You would think things would have moved faster after filing papers regarding the insurance, but now it is almost six months later that we receive the paper work stating the Judge had awarded the insurance policy to me. Doc has to make several phone calls to the court house to determine what needed to be done next. No one seemed to have the answer. The only advice they could give was going to the clerk of courts and have them give us direction as to how to acquire the settlement.

Wednesday January 6th – Another year has come and gone. I went to the court house today to inquire about the life insurance policy. Arriving at the Clerk of Courts, I produced the case file with hopes that someone could answer some questions. After several calls, the lady on duty told me the representative from the financial department was away from her desk I would have to wait for her return call. I stood in the hallway for 25 minutes, all the while thinking this is it, the final peace to the puzzle. Becca was killed, we celebrated her life, and multiple trips to a legal system, decisions made by judges and now the final piece – final payment for her life. Tears came to my eyes as I realized, this in fact really would be the end of any earthly occurrence involving her untimely death. Never would I allow it to be the end of her or what she could have been.

After a period of time, Lauren from the financial department approached me and stated she had just this day received the court order with the judges' decree. She reviewed the amount to be paid, asked for my ID and address so a check could be mailed. Fed-ex would make the final overnight delivery.

Tuesday January 11, 2010 - At approximately 10:10a.m., Fed Ex delivered to my front door the last piece of correspondence that dealt with Becca. 114 weeks and four days after she was murdered, her final life insurance policy benefits were paid and all legal issues closed. You would think I would have been prepared for this, but I feel so empty. The tears fall into my lap as I try to write. I can tell you, I am not ready to let go and do not know when I ever will be. Each day I walk into the serenity room and kiss her good morning, each night before I lay my head on my pillow, I tell her good night, and when I feel that emptiness and need to be near her, I go into her room and sit in the rocker and talk to her.

Sleep my precious baby and know Someday we will meet again in the eternal world God has for us.

CHAPTER SIX

As Life Continues We Go On

Days come and go, work starts and ends, someone is born and someone dies. This is what life is all about. We can withdraw into our self or make a conscious effort to do something productive, to make a difference. I choose to make that difference. Throughout the waiting for trial to happen, I became very involved with the Middle Tennessee YWCA located in Nashville. As a part of my crusade for Becca's memory, I had the opportunity to work with the YWCA and it's wonderful staff to help raise close to $2 million dollars to not only pay off the mortgage to the Weaver Domestic Violence Shelter, but to put monies aside for future needs. One lady I worked with was Mary Jones, who herself was a victim and survived. What a team we made. For her to tell her story about how she managed to get out and then for me to present Becca's story and how her not getting out had impacted my life, couldn't help but impact those we spoke with. Domestic violence is not something that this world should tolerate.

As I move forward in my life, I have returned to school to obtain a degree in Healthcare Administration. I will talk to anyone who will listen about the signs of domestic violence, the help that is there for the asking, and the need for involvement in stopping the cycles. I was honored to receive the 2009 Nashville Coalition Against Domestic Violence Award during the Ceremony on the Bridge and to be able, once again, be supportive to those who had seen the ugliness of such actions. I continue and will continue to support fights and awareness against domestic violence in any arena that I am allowed to do so. You see, I truly believe if Becca hadn't died, she would be the one out here fighting the fight and making a difference, that she would be able to tell her story as Mary has and make a difference in the life of others. I hope to never let her memory die, to be there for another if they need me, and to help raise awareness of domestic violence.

As I try to stay busy, I also remember that grief may set in at any moment, that I probably haven't grieved, but to me, there isn't time for that. There are too many things to do with life for me, for Becca and for anyone who will listen. So, I would like to take the opportunity to share some statistics that many who haven't faced the exposure to domestic violence themselves may not be aware of. It is important to understand this is an epidemic that needs to be controlled, and we have to be the ones to take control.

Domestic Violence Statistics

I would strongly recommend anyone with questions to access the national website (http://www.ncadv.org/files/DomesticViolen ceFactSheet(National).pdf) and also the local domestic violence data base in your area by typing domestic violence statistics and the name of your state.

In order to understand this violence, you must know the signs and symptoms to look for. From WebMD (http://www.webmd. com/mental-health/tc/domestic-violence-signs-of-domestic-violence)

Domestic Violence - Signs of Domestic Violence

Most relationships have difficult times, and almost every couple argues occasionally. But violence is different from common marital or relationship discord. Domestic violence is a pattern of abuse that a partner-former or current partner, spouse, or boyfriend or girlfriend-uses to control the behavior of another.

Domestic violence often starts with threats, name-calling, and slamming doors or breaking dishes, and escalates to pushing, slapping, and other violent acts. See more types of abuse. If you are concerned about your relationship, ask yourself the following questions.

Does your partner:

- Embarrass or belittle you or put you down?
- Say hurtful things to you?
- Dislike your friends and family and discourage your relationships with others?
- Make all the decisions in the relationship?
- Chastise you after social functions for talking with other people?
- Act jealous of people you talk to?
- Blame you for his or her mistakes?
- Try to make you feel worthless or helpless?
- Forbid or prevent you from working or going to school?
- Keep money, credit cards, and checking accounts away from you?
- Control access to your medicines or medical devices?
- Threaten to have you deported?
- Throw dishes or other objects?
- Abuse your children or pet when mad at you?
- Push, slap, kick, or otherwise assault you?
- Demand sex, make you perform sexual acts you are not comfortable with, or sexually assault you?

IF ANY OF THESE BEHAVIORS ARE OCCURRING,
YOU NEED TO SEEK HELP.

Do you have a friend, coworker, relative, or neighbor who you think may be in an abusive relationship? Warning signs that may indicate that a person is a victim of domestic abuse include:

- Bruises or injuries that look like they came from choking, punching, or being thrown down. Black eyes, red or purple marks at the neck, and sprained wrists are common injuries sustained in violent relationships. An injury such as bruised arms might suggest that a victim tried to defend herself.

- Attempting to hide bruises with makeup or clothing.
- Making excuses like tripping or being accident-prone or clumsy. Often the seriousness of the injury does not match up with the explanation.
- Having low self-esteem; being extremely apologetic and meek.
- Referring to the partner's temper but not disclosing extent of abuse.
- Having few close friends and being isolated from relatives and coworkers and kept from making friends.
- Having little money available; may not have credit cards or even a car.
- Having a drug or alcohol abuse problem.
- Having symptoms of depression, such as sadness or hopelessness, or loss of interest in daily activities.
- Talking about suicide or attempting suicide. For more information, see <u>warning signs of suicide</u>.

ENCOURAGE THIS PERSON TO TALK WITH
A HEALTH PROFESSIONAL.

Healthwise Incorporated. Reprinted with permission. This information is not intended to replace the advice of a doctior. Healthwise disclaims any liability for your use of this information.

I would also like to provide to you some statistics and information from some of the national websites, with the idea of increasing awareness of the true impact domestic violence has on our nation as a whole. This includes web addresses for you to visit for further details.

Bureau of Justice Statistics (http://www.ojp.usdoj.gov/bjs/intimate/ipv.htm) list:

Violence between intimates includes -
homicides, rapes, robberies, and assaults committed by intimates.

Intimate relationships involve -
current or former spouses, boyfriends, or girlfriends, including same sex relationships.

Intimates are distinguished from -
- other relatives (parent, child, sibling, grandparent, in-law, cousin)
- acquaintances (friend, co-worker, neighbor, schoolmate, someone known)
- strangers (anyone not previously known by the victim)

Domestic violence includes -
intimate partner violence as well as violence between family members.

Violence between intimates is difficult to measure --
because it often occurs in private, and victims are often reluctant to report incidents to anyone because of shame or fear of reprisal.

Sources:

National Crime Victimization Survey (NCVS). See also NCVS methodology.

Supplementary Homicide Reports (SHR) of the FBI's Uniform

Crime Reporting Program (UCR) as presented in Homicide Trends in the United States

American Bar Association (http://www.abanet.org/domviol/ statistics.html) provides:

- In a 1995-1996 study conducted in the 50 States and the District of Columbia, nearly 25% of women and 7.6% of men were raped and/or physically assaulted by a current or former spouse, cohabiting partner, or dating partner/acquaintance at some time in their lifetime (based on survey of 16,000 participants, equally male and female).

  Patricia Tjaden & Nancy Thoennes, U.S. Dep't of Just., NCJ 181867, *Extent, Nature, and Consequences of Intimate Partner Violence, at iii (2000)*, available at http://www.ojp.usdoj.gov/nij/pubs-sum/181867.htm

- Approximately 1.3 million women and 835,000 men are physically assaulted by an intimate partner annually in the United States.

  Patricia Tjaden & Nancy Thoennes, U.S. Dep't of Just., NCJ 183781, *Full Report of the Prevalence, Incidence, and Consequences of Intimate Partner Violence Against Women: Findings from the National Violence Against Women Survey, at iv* (2000), available at http://www. ojp.usdoj.gov/nij/pubs-sum/183781.htm

- Intimate partner violence made up 20% of all nonfatal violent crime experienced by women in 2001.

Callie Marie Rennison, U.S. Dep't of Just., NCJ 197838, Bureau of Justice Statistics Crime Data Brief: Intimate Partner Violence, 1993-2001, at 1 (2003), available at http://www.ojp.usdoj.gov/bjs/pub/pdf/ipv01.pdf

- Intimate partners committed 3% of the nonfatal violence against men.

Callie Marie Rennison, U.S. Dep't of Just., NCJ 197838, *Bureau of Justice Statistics Crime Data Brief: Intimate Partner Violence, 1993-2001, at 1* (2003), available at http://www.ojp.usdoj.gov/bjs/pub/pdf/ipv01.pdf

- In 2000, 1,247 women and 440 men were killed by an intimate partner. In recent years, an intimate partner killed approximately 33% of female murder victims and 4% of male murder victims.

Callie Marie Rennison, U.S. Dep't of Just., NCJ 197838, *Bureau of Justice Statistics Crime Data Brief: Intimate Partner Violence, 1993-2001, at 1* (2003), available at http://www.ojp.usdoj.gov/bjs/pub/pdf/ipv01.pdf

- Access to firearms yields a more than five-fold increase in risk of intimate partner homicide when considering other factors of abuse, according to a recent study, suggesting that abusers who possess guns tend to inflict the most severe abuse on their partners.

Jacquelyn C. Campbell et al., *Risk Factors For Femicide in Abusive Relationships: Results From A Multi-Site Case Control Study, 93 Am. J. of Public Health 1089, 1092*

(2003), abstract available at http://www.ajph.org/cgi/content/abstract/93/7/1089

- Of females killed with a firearm, almost two-thirds were killed by their intimate partners. The number of females shot and killed by their husband or intimate partner was more than three times higher than the total number murdered by male strangers using all weapons combined in single victim/single offender incidents in 2002.

  The Violence Pol'y Ctr., *When Men Murder Women: An Analysis of 2002 Homicide Data: Females Murdered by Males in Single Victim/Single Offender Incidents, at 7 (2004)*, available at http://www.vpc.org/studies/wmmw2004.pdf

According to the U.S. Department of Justice, between 1998 and 2002:

- Of the almost 3.5 million violent crimes committed against family members, 49% of these were crimes against spouses.
- 84% of spouse abuse victims were females, and 86% of victims of dating partner abuse at were female.
- Males were 83% of spouse murderers and 75% of dating partner murderers
- 50% of offenders in state prison for spousal abuse had killed their victims. Wives were more likely than husbands to be killed by their spouses: wives were about half of all spouses in the population in 2002, but 81% of all persons killed by their spouse.

Matthew R. Durose et al., U.S. Dep't of Just., NCJ 207846, *Bureau of Justice Statistics, Family Violence Statistics: Including Statistics on Strangers and Acquaintances, at 31-32 (2005),* available at http:// www.ojp.usdoj.gov/bjs/pub/pdf/fvs.pdf

The National Women's Study, a three-year longitudinal study of a national probability sample of 4,008 adult women (2,008 of whom represent a cross section of all adult women and 2,000 of whom are an over sample of younger women between the ages of 18 and 34), found:

- 13% of adult women had been victims of completed rape during their lifetime
- 22% of rape victims were assaulted by someone they had never seen before or did not know well.
- 9% of victims were raped by husbands or ex-husbands.
- 11% were raped by fathers or stepfathers.
- 10% were raped by boyfriends or ex-boyfriends.
- 16% were raped by other relatives.
- 29% were raped by other non-relatives, such as friends and neighbors.

See Dean G. Kilpatrick et al., *Rape in America: A Report to the Nation* (1992); Heidi S. Resnick et al., *Prevalence of Civilian Trauma and PTSD in a Representative National Sample of Women, 61 J. of Consulting and Clinical Psychol. 984 (1993);* Dean G. Kilpatrick et al., *A 2-Year Longitudinal Analysis of the Relationship Between Violent Assault and Substance Use in Women, 65 J. of Consulting and Clinical Psychol. 834 (1997);* Kilpatrick et al., *Rape, Other Violence Against Women, and Posttraumatic Stress Disorder: Critical Issues in Assessing the Adversity-Stress-Psychopathology Relationship, in Adversity, Stress, & Psychopathology 161-176* (Bruce P. Dohrenwend ed., 1998); Dean G. Kilpatrick, *Rape and Sexual Assault, Aug. 7, 2006,* http://www.musc.edu/vawprevention/research/sa.shtml

Domestic Violence & Children

- Slightly more than half of female victims of intimate violence live in households with children under age 12.

  Lawrence A. Greenfield et al.,U.S. Dep't of Just., NCJ 167237, *Violence by Intimates: Analysis of Data on Crimes by Current or Former Spouse, Boyfriends, and Girlfriends* (1998) available at www.ojp.usdoj.gov/bjs/pub/pdf/vi.pdf

- A recent study of low-income pre-school children in Michigan found that nearly half (46.7 percent) of the children in the study had been exposed to at least one incident of mild or severe violence in the family. Children who had been exposed to violence suffered symptoms of post-traumatic stress disorder, such as bed-wetting or nightmares, and were at greater risk than their peers of having allergies, asthma, gastrointestinal problems, headaches and flu.

  Sandra Graham-Bermann & Julie Seng, *Violence Exposure and Traumatic Stress Symptoms as Additional Predictors of Health Problems in High-Risk Children,* 146 J. of Pediatrics 309 (2005).

- Battered women are not the only victims of abuse - it is estimated that anywhere between 3.3 million and 10 million children witness domestic violence annually. Research demonstrates that exposure to violence can have serious negative effects on children's development.

Sharmila Lawrence, National Center for Children in Poverty, Domestic Violence and Welfare Policy: *Research Findings That Can Inform Policies on Marriage and Child Well-Being* 5 (2002).

- One study of 2,245 children and teenagers found that recent exposure to violence in the home was a significant factor in predicting a child's violent behavior.

Mark I. Singer, et al., Cuyahoga County Cmty. Health Research Institute, *The Mental Health Consequences of Children's Exposure to Violence* (1998).

- Children exposed to Intimate Partner Violence were 1.6 times as likely to score in the borderline to clinical level range on externalizing behaviors relative to children of similar age and sex (as measured on three scales of internalizing behaviors, externalizing behaviors, and social competence according to the standardized psychometric instrument of Achenbach's Child Behavior Checklist, or CBCL).

Mary A. Kernic et al., *Behavioral Problems Among Children Whose Mothers are Abused by an Intimate*

Partner, 27 Child Abuse & Neglect 1231 at 1239 (2003).

- Children exposed to maternal Intimate Partner Violence, without experiencing child maltreatment, were 40% more likely to have a total behavioral problem score within the borderline to clinical range than CBCL normative children.

Mary A. Kernic et al., *Behavioral Problems Among Children Whose Mothers are Abused by an Intimate Partner,* 27 Child Abuse & Neglect 1231 at 1239 (2003).

See also Family Violence Prevention Fund, *The Facts on Children and Domestic Violence,* (2005), available at http://endabuse.org/resources/facts/Children.pdf (Aug 1, 2005).

Just from these few sources, you can see the impact of domestic violence in our society. We as a nation need to get involved and help protect our children, our mothers, our daughters, our fellow human beings and find a way to stop this cycle of violence. If you are a victim, please call the below listed number for help from professionals and law enforcement or if you have a friend or loved one being abused, the hotline can still help answer your questions. They are there for all of us.

NATIONAL DOMESTIC VIOLENCE HOTLINE

1-800-799-SAFE (7233)
1-800-787-3224 (TTY)

Promise Yourself

To be so strong that nothing can disturb
  your peace of mind.
To talk health, happiness and prosperity to
  every person you meet
To make all your friends feel that there is
  something in them.
To look at the sunny side of everything and
  make your optimism come true.
To think only of the best and expect only
  the best.
To be just as enthusiastic about the success
  of others as you are about your own.
To forget the mistakes of the past and press
  on to the greater achievements of the future.
To wear a cheerful countenance at all times
  and give every living creature you meet a smile.
To give so much time to the improvement of
  yourself that you have no time to criticize
others.
To be too large for worry, too noble for anger,
  too strong for fear, and too happy to
  permit the presence of trouble

Author Unknown

93

End Notes

CHAPTER ONE: THE BEGINNING NOVEMBER 2007

1 - Dyer KA. Take Care to Cope with Loss and Grief. Retrieved May 16, 2010, from Journey of Hearts, http://www.jourmeyofhearts.org

2 – Stephens, Simon. Grief Support after the Death of a Child. Retrieved May 16, 2010, from http://www.compassionatefriends.org/home.aspx

CHAPTER TWO: CELEBRATION OF LIFE

1 – Reprinted by permission. Grace for the Moment. Max Luckadoo, 2007, Thomas Nelson Inc. Nashville, Tennessee. All rights reserved.

Scripture taken from King James and New King James Version noted per verse